Acrobat to Zebra
A Journey Through the Alphabet

Collected and illustrated by Bettina Guthridge

CELEBRATION PRESS
Pearson Learning Group

A a

acrobat   airplane   albatross   alligator   anaconda   ant
antelope   apples   armadillo   asteroids   avocado   axe

baboon   basketball   beetles   berries   bicycle   birds
boat   brachiosaurus   bridge   bumblebee   butterfly

C c

cactus   calendar   camel   canary   caribou   caterpillar
cheetah   clouds   cockatoo   comet   crayons   crocodile

D d

daffodil   desk   dish   dog   dolphin   donkey   dove
dragon   dragonfly   drum   drumsticks   duck

E e

eagle   ear   earthworm   easel   echidna   eel   eggs
eggshell   eight   elephant   elk   elm   emu   eyelashes

F f

fan   feather   fern   fin   fingers   fireworks   fish   five
flamingo   flies   flowers   flute   forest   fox   frog   fur

G g

garden   gecko   giraffe   gloves   goat   goldfish   goose
gorilla   grapes   grasshopper   greenhouse   guitar

H h

hammock   handkerchief   harp   hat   hawk   hay   hedgehog
helicopter   hen   hippopotamus   hopscotch   hummingbird   hyena

I i

ibis   iceberg   ice cream   icicles   igloo   iguana
impala   ink   insect   Inuit   iris   island   ivy

J j

jackal   jack-in-the-box   jaguar   jeans   jelly beans
jewelry   jigsaw puzzle   jug   jumbo jet   jungle

K k

kaleidoscope kangaroo kayak kettle key keyhole
kingfisher kite kitten kiwi koala kookaburra

L l

ladder   ladybug   lake   lantern   leaves   leopard
lighthouse   lightning   lily   lion   lizard   lotus

M m

marbles   mask   mittens   monkey   moon   moose

mosquito   moth   mountain   mouse   mushroom

N n

nails   neck   necklace   nectarine   needle   nest   net
newspaper   nightingale   nose   notebook   numbat

O o

oak   oar   oboe   observatory   ocean   octagon   octopus
orange   orangutang   orchid   osprey   otter   owl

P p

pajamas   panda   parakeet   peacock   penguin   pentagon
pig   pillow   platypus   polar bear   porcupine   possum

Q q

quail   quarters   quartz   queen   question mark
quicksand   quill   quilt   quince

R r

raccoon   racquet   rainbow   rat   rattlesnake   rectangle
rhinoceros   ribbon   ring   rocket   rollerblades

S s

sails   sandcastle   scorpion   seagull   seashells   shark
sky   snake   snorkel   spider   squares   starfish   sunset

T t

tail   tambourine   teepee   telescope   ten   tiger   toadstool
tortoise   tower   train   triangle   trumpet   tunnel   turtle

U u   V v

UFO   ukelele   umbrella   unicorn   unicycle

vase   veranda   violets   violin   volcano   vulture

W w

walrus   wasp   watch   waves   web   whale   wheelbarrow
wheelchair   window   wing   wolf   wombat

Xx Yy Zz

x-ray   xylophone

yacht   yak   yogurt   yo-yo

zebra   zigzag   zippers   zither   zoo